Persuasion

----- ✑❦✑❦ -----

The definitive guide to Understanding Influence, Mind Control, and NLP

Ryan James

© Copyright 2017 by Ryan James - All rights reserved.

The following Book is reproduced below with the goal of providing information that is as accurate and as reliable as possible. Regardless, purchasing this Book can be seen as consent to the fact that both the publisher and the author of this book are in no way experts on the topics discussed within, and that any recommendations or suggestions made herein are for entertainment purposes only. Professionals should be consulted as needed before undertaking any of the action endorsed herein.

This declaration is deemed fair and valid by both the American Bar Association and the Committee of Publishers Association and is legally binding throughout the United States.

Furthermore, the transmission, duplication or reproduction of any of the following work, including precise information, will be considered an illegal act, irrespective whether it is done electronically or in print. The legality extends to creating a secondary or tertiary copy of the work or a recorded copy and is only allowed with express written consent of the Publisher. All additional rights are reserved.

The information in the following pages is broadly considered to be a truthful and accurate account of facts, and as such any inattention, use or misuse of the information in question by the reader will render any resulting actions solely under their purview. There are no scenarios in which the publisher or the original author of this work can be in any fashion deemed liable for any hardship or damages that may befall them after undertaking information described herein.

Additionally, the information found on the following pages is intended for informational purposes only and should thus be considered, universal. As befitting its nature, the information presented is without assurance regarding its continued validity or interim quality. Trademarks that mentioned are done without written consent and can in no way be considered an endorsement from the trademark holder.

Table of Contents

Introduction 1

Chapter 1: The Art of Persuasion 3

Chapter 2: Understanding, And How to Use It 11

Chapter 3: Using Influence 17

Chapter 4: Mind Control 25

Chapter 5: NLP (Neuro-Linguistic Programming) 37

Chapter 6: Reflect on Yourself 55

Conclusion 67

© Copyright 2016 by Ryan James - All rights reserved.

The follow eBook is reproduced below with the goal of providing information that is as accurate and reliable as possible. Regardless, purchasing this eBook is as consent to the fact that both the publisher and the author of this book are in no way experts on the topics discussed within and that any recommendations or suggestions that are made herein are for entertainment purposes only. Professionals should be consulted as needed prior to undertaking any of the action endorsed herein.

This declaration is deemed fair and valid by both the American Bar Association and the Committee of Publishers Association and is legally binding throughout the United States.

Furthermore, the transmission, duplication or reproduction of any of the following work including specific information will be considered an illegal act irrespective of if it is done electronically or in print. This extends to creating a secondary or tertiary copy of the work or a recorded copy and is only allowed with express written consent from the Publisher. All additional right reserved.

The information in the following pages is broadly considered to be a truthful and accurate account of facts and as such any inattention, use or misuse of the information in question by the reader will render any resulting actions solely under their purview. There are no scenarios in which the publisher or the original author of this work can be in any fashion deemed liable for any hardship or damages that may befall them after undertaking information described herein.

Additionally, the information in the following pages is intended only for informational purposes and should thus be thought of as universal. As befitting its nature, it is presented without assurance regarding its prolonged validity or interim quality. Trademarks that are mentioned are done without written consent and can in no way be considered an endorsement from the trademark holder.

Introduction

Congratulations on downloading this book, and thank you for doing so.

This book is about the power you hold within you, and how to use that power to get what you want out of your life. The art of persuasion can aid you in reaching any goal, of changing the minds of both yourself, and others, and can be the beginning of any positive change. You are in charge, and you already hold the keys to success. You just need to understand what those keys and skills are, and how to use them.

The following book, and the chapters contained within, will discuss and introduce you to the fine arts of persuasion, understanding, influence, mind control, and NLP (or Neuro Linguistic Programming). This book will explain how to use

Introduction

and utilize these tools in everyday application to your advantage, and how to become better at using these skills to attain any goal you hope to. You will learn what these skills are, how they work, the benefits of possessing these skill sets, and how to improve your abilities. Practical applications for use of these skills is possible, and with knowledge, comes power. With power, comes achieving your goals and getting what you want out of your life.

There are a vast array of books and literature on the subjects we will go over in this book on the market today, thank you again for choosing this one! Every effort was made to ensure this book is full of as much useful information and practical applications as possible, please enjoy!

Chapter 1:

The Art of Persuasion

Persuasion is a powerful tool. If you can persuade another person that you are right, anything is possible. But first, let's start with the basics. What is persuasion? Persuasion, or the act of persuading, is the ability to change another's way of thinking by convincing the other individual that your belief, which is grounded on assurance, is correct. Assurance can be making a declaration and not just a statement. Being confident in your words, thoughts, and ideas exudes self-confidence. People are more apt to listen to someone who makes assertions in a confident manner. But, to have the self-assurance needed to persuade another person, knowledge is required. You must know what you are speaking about with

Chapter 1: The Art of Persuasion

authority for others to concede to your ideas or wants. Whatever the end-goal is, you need to know a lot about it. Do your homework and be ready to explain why you are correct. It is important to note, that authority does not equal pushy. In fact, being too pushy or in-your-face with someone is a huge turn-off, and will often be met with immediate rejection of your idea or desire.

There are many ways to persuade another person that your way of thinking is right, and there also many degrees of persuasion one can use, from a subtle suggestion, to outright pressure. Swaying someone to think like you do, to see things your way, is useful and doesn't necessarily mean they need to be coerced. Sometimes, people want to be one the same page as you, they just need a little help getting there!

So, how do you convince another person that they should agree with you, or do what you want, for both their benefit and your own?

Persuasion

The first step is understanding that to persuade an individual, they should be open to listening to you. Someone that has no desire to hear you out will not be open to the conversation necessary to understand where you are coming from, and why you feel or think as you do. Your target audience is someone that is willing to hear you out, think about what you are saying, and be open to your suggestion. Knowing who you are trying to persuade is key. To reach your audience, whether it's your significant other or a room full of peers, you should know others inside and out, front to back. If you are interacting with someone who is passive and meek, tone down your voice and use less aggressive language. If you want to convince your very outgoing friend that your plan is more desirable than theirs, turn up the vocal volume and get amped when you speak about what you want. In fact, it is important to keep in mind that who you are trying to persuade is another human, just like you, and not a target or opponent. People want and crave connection. Being persuasive isn't

Chapter 1: The Art of Persuasion

about winning someone else over, or beating them, it is about convincing them that you only want what is best for them and yourself. Individuals you have regular conversations with, or people that you have already formed a relationship with are easier to persuade and more open to your ideas as there is already a relationship base in place. These are people that you engage and connect with about any number of things. You understand what is important to them, how they prioritize their lives, and what makes them tick. Using what you know about another person is vital.

Other small tactics that are useful when trying to be persuasive are subtle compliments. Being genuine in your compliment is the goal, overt flattery makes others feel like you are fake. And being fake will not get you far. Rather than complementing someone for their appearance or a materialistic nicety, compliment them on their brain. Saying things like, "You know a lot about the topic", rather than "Oh, I love your hairstyle", make for more meaningful and respectful interactions. Utilizing positive words, rather than negative language also help set the tone for the conversation. Saying words like "empathize, understand," and using phrases like, "I agree, however", or "I appreciate your opinion, but", are non-aggressive yet firm ways to let the other party know that while you may not agree with their idea or opinion, you understand their thought process and appreciate their opinions.

Now that we understand the basics of persuading someone you know, what about persuading someone who you have never met before? You obviously won't know this person on a deeper level, and knowing their motivations at first sight isn't an option, so how do we get those we don't know on our side?

People tend to lean their opinions or beliefs systems towards people they like. The easiest way to get someone to like you, is for them to feel like YOU like THEM. Engage with someone you don't know with your whole being, turn

Chapter 1: The Art of Persuasion

physically toward them, smile, and express interest in them and what they have to say. Use your nonverbal body queues to express your interest in them. Introduce yourself, and be open to being vulnerable. The more another person knows about you, the more they are willing to divulge about themselves. When they are speaking, don't just hear them. Listen. Listening as a means to reply is felt, and somehow, people always no when you aren't listening to their words, but merely waiting for your chance to respond. If you make the interaction all about you, you will be met with rejection almost immediately. Show your interest and excitement about meeting someone new, allow them the floor as much as possible, and wait. The more you listen, the more they talk. The more they talk, the more you learn. And, the more you learn about someone, the more you understand them.

Another tactic to persuade another person to agree with you is touch. Not aggressive hand-holding, or high-fives, but often a simple touch of your finger on their upper arm in a quick and nondescript manner creates a huge physiological response in the human body. Chemicals are released in the brain, signaling a sign of embrace, acceptance, and often is barely registered. Timing is key when reaching out to someone who is almost virtually unknown to you. If you choose to try this technique of persuasion, the execution needs to be after the initial greeting has given way to positive feedback and conversation. Making sure to be looking the other person in the face, and being swift and confident in your gesture makes it feel more natural, and not an invasion of personal space. It gives a sense of welcoming, the budding of understanding and even friendship.

When considering persuasion, it is always best to remember that practice and practical application only makes you more persuasive.

Chapter 2:

Understanding, And How to Use It

To get what you want from other's, you need to be able to understand them. Now, this is easy when dealing with family, friends, coworkers, and people you have daily or regular contact with. You talk about a myriad of things, know what they think and feel, and why they feel as they do. And if you don't understand them, it isn't hard to ask. Relationships that have already been established make for easier understanding, you "get them" and where they are coming from, so persuading someone you know is not always that hard of a feat. New acquaintances, people you have never encountered before, whether you are trying to sale them something, or give a talk, now that is

Chapter 2: Understanding, And How to Use It

much more difficult. With no base to go on, how does one convince another to agree? Well, the most important detail is figuring out who your target audience is, what you think they may feel, and make initial contact all about them.

Humans are a self-absorbed species. We spend most of our time thinking about our lives. What do we want, how do we get it, who do we love and care for, how's our financial health, are we feeling okay physically? It goes without saying that most of us are consistently absorbed with thoughts of our own lives and we are driven based on our own circumstances. So, how do we get to know someone quickly so that we may create the relationship base needed to be able to persuade them?

We talk about them, with them!

Whether speaking before an audience, or trying to sell a product to the public, the easiest way to get to know someone is to get them talking about themselves. Asking open ended questions that can't end with a yes or no answer, listening to them, vesting your time and total attention to them, and engaging allows others to open up about themselves. The more we know about another person, the more we understand who they are, what they believe, and how we can go about persuading them to agree with us. We need to be able to understand their motivations, and appeal to those things specifically.

An effective way to get another to talk about themselves is to ask a question, and wait. After the individual answers the question you posed to them, do not reply immediately. Pause, making eye contact, and wait a second or two before speaking or responding back. Humans often feel compelled to fill empty silences, and many times when we wait a moment before replying or asking a follow up question, an individual will continue speaking to fill the space. Try it out! This tactic does not always work, and can make for an awkward silence, so timing silence is key. Wait too long, and both you and the other party

Chapter 2: Understanding, And How to Use It

will feel a little out of place, but waiting just a beat or two often compels the other person to fill the silence. This gives you even more knowledge than you asked for, and can only benefit you and your goals.

Since it is mentioned in the last paragraph, let's go over timing and its importance when considering persuasion.

Timing is of the utmost importance, and not just during a conversation. When trying to appeal to an individual or audience, the timing of persuasion and the reason for it is key. If you want to sell something, steer the conversation towards the future. What one does not have now, they may soon need and be left wanting. It is better to buy now, and save the risk of not having what they need when they need it. If arguing a case, or debating about why your opinion is correct, steer the conversation to the past. Using examples of previous let downs or negative outcomes, and why your opinion or idea will prevent the past from repeating itself is a very compelling idea. Nobody wants to feel negative emotions like foolishness, stupidity, or ignorance. A good way to get others to open to your way of thought is by the simple but effective reminder that repeating mistakes of the past is unavoidable, unless a change is made. And you can offer that change by way of your ideas, thoughts, or actions. If giving a presentation, utilize the present state of things. Going over what is happening now and what the current issues are is a good and effective lead in to discuss what has happened in the past, and what may happen in the future. Using the present, past, and future examples as a base for your ideas makes for a compelling and effective argument.

Remember, that while timing is key, it is hard for someone to argue logic. Know your facts, know your goals, and know how you want to get there. Appealing to one's sense of logic appeals to one's sense of intelligence. People want to feel like they are making a smart decision, and you can

Chapter 2: Understanding, And How to Use It

offer them that. There are other individuals who base their choices on emotion. Once you understand what makes them feel, you can use it to your advantage to convince them that you know exactly how they feel, and you can help them. Another final aspect to consider is your authority on what you want people to agree with. Your authority can be your expertise, your experiences, or even just the way you carry yourself and appear. Be confident, know what you want, and learn to understand how to get others to agree with you by understanding the way they think. If it is important to them, it is important to you. You are now already on the same page about one thing, and a base is now created to build the trust needed for them to empathize and agree with what you think.

Chapter 3:

Using Influence

Influence is a powerful, but often subtle tool. The ability to affect or change someone's opinion, or create a change in circumstances without forcing the change directly is an art form all its own. Creating changes or conditions as situations develop creates lasting impact. It can make others sit up and take notice of you and your presence, and often create a perception of you that may make others want to defer to you in the future. In this chapter, we will go over how to create influence, how to build your skills in regards to influencing others, and how to utilize the influence you have built to achieve your goals.

Chapter 3: Using Influence

Influence is based on basic, but key factors. Let's start with a room full of people whom you do not know. Your entrance into this room is vital. You may not know anyone, but not everyone present will know this. Presenting yourself in the most flattering way within the first few seconds will often dictate the way everyone in the room sees you. Smile as you enter the room, walking with your back and head in straight but relaxed alignment. Taking time not to rush or enter too slowly, imagine you are just walking into a room in your home. An often-effective trick to make you seem more approachable is to give a short wave, as if you are acknowledging someone you know. This makes others assume that someone else in the room already knows you, and that in and of itself makes you seem more likeable or interesting.

When first meeting someone, making eye contact and firmly shaking their hand while smiling boosts your effective charisma with the other individual. Charisma is more about how you make the other person feel when they are in your presence. Charisma is not necessarily about being the life of the party. To work on your charisma, first consider your own strengths. Are you humorous? Are you already outgoing and friendly? Do you tend to be shy and quieter? You can use any of your strengths to your advantage, it is all about understanding how to use them. If you are more of an introvert, pick one or two people off to the side of the crowd or room to engage with. When initiating communication, use your quieter presence to let others do more of the talking, and only steer the conversation in the direction you want it to go into when necessary. As we have established previously, people love to talk about themselves! If you are outgoing, place yourself in a position of power, feel free to approach larger groupings of people and greet them. Again, use your strengths to your advantage.

Chapter 3: Using Influence

People that hold sway over others can attest, influence is all about give and take. When people feel, a relationship is based on reciprocation, they trust the relationship easier and sooner, and have less reservations. Try asking a small favor of someone, and then in turn offering them the same in return. An example would be offering to hold someone's place in line while they use the restroom, taking notes for them while they excuse themselves momentarily during a meeting or presentation, and then asking them to do the same for you upon their return. This give and take lays a foundation of comradery, like you and the other party are already friendly. And people that feel like you like them, like you in return.

Building relationships overnight is not easy, but it can be easier by being friendly. Smiling and eye contact play a role in how you make other people feel. If you project that you are happy to see others, that you are happy to be speaking with them, they will in turn feel happy to be communicating with you. Your body language speaks volumes, and others pick up on what you are conveying with yours, even if they aren't fully aware of it. When engaging with another, take note in how they are standing or sitting. If they are standing with their arms at their sides, you should mimic their stance. Mimicking someone's body language is another way of building an unspoken but solid foundation. If they are clearly exhibiting stress, mimic their stance. An example of this would be if their arms are crossed over the front of their body in defensive pose. After a few minutes of conversation, move your arms to a more relaxed and natural position. In most instances, the person you are communicating with will subconsciously reposition their body language to mimic your own. This is an example of how you are already gaining influence and trust with someone who you barely know.

Chapter 3: Using Influence

When talking to individuals you want to gain influence over, another aspect to consider is your own attitude towards them. We know that our physical body language plays a role, and that reciprocating is important as well, but just as important is how you project yourself. Greeting another with a smile is great, but now that the conversation has started, maintain a neutral but relaxed facial expression. Staying involved and being attentive when others speak again makes them feel good speaking with you. Asking questions per the flow of conversation shows that you are listening to them, and everyone wants to be heard. Being respectful, calm, and diplomatic in your interactions makes you more friendly and approachable. Showing gratitude for their time, and being appreciated will encourage others to appreciate your attention and time in return.

A good way to connect with others is to be authentic in your communications with them. You want to convey that you are sincere, that you are invested in what is important to them. Finding common ground and things that you can easily agree on leads to topics that they are more emotionally connected to. Be emotionally curious by asking questions that will elicit an emotional opinion or feeling from the other party. This helps you understand what is important to them, and therefore how to exert your influence with them on not just by using a logical stance, but by an emotional appeal.

A final consideration to help you influence others is people's desire to belong. People want to feel like they are part of a group or movement, that they are included and belong with their peers. When you express authority on a topic or opinion or desire, support your stance with evidence. Statements that include others who agree with you, or statistical facts that indicate trends within the topic, make others pause and consider who else agrees with you, why your opinion is accurate or right, and why they too should align their opinions with your own.

Chapter 3: Using Influence

Once you have established a base relationship with another person, whether it be simple and basic, or deep and complex, influencing them is not that difficult. If you are met with resistance, ask more questions. Many times, people resist an idea or a change for many reasons than those that rest on the surface. Express a desire to know why they do not agree, empathize with their reasons for resistance, and listen to why they hesitate. Often, once you understand why they reject your influence, you can redirect or discuss other viable reasons for them to change their viewpoint for your benefit, and theirs too.

Chapter 4:

Mind Control

Mind control sounds like a devious plot in a movie, but you have most likely experienced it many times a day for many years and never noticed it. Mind control, or the idea of thought-reform, is a controversial theory and practice, but one that does not necessarily mean tricking and scheming. As a matter of fact, mind control can be as simple as subliminal suggestion used to steer one in the direction you want rather than the direction they were going autonomously.

There are many schools of thought in regards to mind control, but for this book, let's look at a common example of mind control to start. Color, smell, sight, sound, and taste are used on the consumer by every company selling a

Chapter 4: Mind Control

product to advance their customers and sales. When you enter your local grocery store, often there are fresh cut flowers at the entrance. Now, how often have you bought those flowers? Chances are, never, if maybe a time or two because you forgot a special occasion. Grocers use the presence of these flowers as a means of manipulating the subconscious of their customers. Fresh cut flowers are, well, fresh. Ripe. Pleasant. They subliminally convey they thought of freshness, and your local grocery store wants you to be thinking about all the fresh produce they have waiting for you. More often, these grocers make more on the sale of their fresh produce over name brand canned and frozen produce, and if you buy the produce they have available, more of your dollars go in their pocket as opposed to mass production companies.

Every day, you are exposed to one form of mind control or another. Product placement on television and in movies. The music you hear in

Persuasion

a store or even an elevator. Friends that are so convincing, you can't help but agree, or you find yourself always saying yes to them. In this chapter, we will go over some techniques of mind control, also known as coercive persuasion, and how you can achieve goals by using these techniques to your advantage.

Re-education is a very optimal, but controversial tool in mind control. The ability to re-educate another person's previous thought process or beliefs is possible, but can take time. At the heart of re-education sits repetition. I repeat, repetition. By repeating the same belief, idea, or thought to another person, repeatedly, you are impressing upon them the change from their own ideas towards your own. And this repetition leads to immersion in the idea or action you want them to follow. Being immersed in an idea, the idea in question always being repeated, the idea or goal always being spoken of, leads to the individual re-examining their previous feelings about the issue. Re-examining one's feelings

Chapter 4: Mind Control

often leads to them coming to a new conclusion. Your conclusion. You have just exerted a form of mind control on another individual, and now they agree with you.

Priming an individual is another effective way to get what you want. Some who see this activity negatively may refer to in as indoctrination, but the goal is not to necessarily start a cult. You are just trying to get others to agree with you, and are trying to use all the available tools you possess to your advantage. Priming involves softening a person towards you and your ideas, easing them into the thought that you know what is best. Softening can include hours of conversation, empathizing with them and showing them that you care or love them. You care about what happens, you understand them. Once you have a foundation of trust through understanding and priming, soft persuasion towards the new idea, belief, or action can be introduced. It is imperative that you have formed a mutual bond or respect with the person

Persuasion

who you want to influence. And it is a given that change takes time.

A few techniques to help you on your path to persuasion using coercion may involve thinking for others, being specific in your logic and requests, creating a real sense of urgency, and stressing the importance of your goal or idea. When presenting someone with a change in long held ideas or requests, thinking for them takes the pressure of deciding off them. People often have enough on their mental plates as it is, you shouldn't be asking them to take on more, especially when you can do the heavy lifting for them. Explain exactly why they should see things your way, offering as many examples as possible as to the correctness to your idea, proof that what you want is not only right, but it is proven to be effective or accurate. Once you have specifically lined out why they should agree with you, tell them what is next and why things need to be done your way. Be friendly but as firm and confident in your pitch to them as you

Chapter 4: Mind Control

need be, and often discouraging questions until you are finished explaining your stance helps steer others in your direction. They often forget their questions or objections as they listen to you explain what you want, why, and what you think needs to happen next to achieve the goal. It is all about the goal.

While we are on the subject of your goals and what you want to achieve, it is imperative to stress the importance of what you want to achieve. If others are consistently being spoken with on how important the idea or goal is, and specifics on why it is so important, eventually they start to see your idea as more than just something you want, but an issue of utmost importance. Your thought or goal becomes something more, and it should be more to you too. it should be a movement. A goal doesn't have to be a social ideal to be a movement, you just need others to feel it's importance as much as you do. Everyone wants to be on the right side of history, no matter how big or small the

Persuasion

issue is. And all it takes is someone to see your want as a matter that needs to be addressed or adjusted, and where there is one person who agrees with you, there are two, and more soon to follow.

So, your idea, goal, or thought is now more than just something you want. Other people want it too. And it is not just important, it is imperative. And it needs to happen now. Creating a sense of urgency is another effective form of utilizing mind control techniques to your benefit. Making urgent statements, or claiming that this situation is time sensitive will create an emotional response in those you wish to influence or persuade. A specific deadline needs to be in place, but the idea that this can't wait long needs to be an underlying sentiment. The quicker you get other people on board, the more important you convince them your want is, the more urgent they believe things are, the less resistance you will run into. As it was mentioned previously, repeating equals results. The more information

Chapter 4: Mind Control

backing your idea or goal people are given, the more likely they will let you think for them and just go with the flow. The more urgent the matter is, the less time people have to ask discouraging questions or second guess their shift in ideas.

Being consistent is the most important aspect of implementing mind control techniques to get what you want. Consistently repeating what you want, and be consistent when rejecting old ideas or goals. Be consistent when speaking about what needs to happen, when and why. These factors should be underlined, in bold print, repeated regularly, and the time sensitivity need to be stressed.

There is nothing wrong with being a little pushy to get what you want out of your life. Another great technique when using mind control is to ask small things of others, or asking for small changes in another's ideas, and then expanding from there. Let's use a raise from your employer as an example. If you want a decent increase in

Persuasion

pay, don't ask for your top dollar pay increase. Ask for a small increase in pay based on your performance and loyalty. Your boss will agree (considering you are worthy of the raise to begin with) and think that they got off cheap keeping you happy. After you have reached the first step in reaching your ultimate pay goal, ask for more work. Let your employer know you are more than happy taking on more responsibility. You can possibly save them money if you are doing more work than before, they may not have to hire another employee to work weekends if you are willing to come in for a few hours on a Saturday. Now, you have a pay increase, but you have more responsibility. It only seems fair that you are paid a little more now that you are a more valuable resource for your employer to utilize. It's better they give you another slight pay increase to cover your knowledge and expertise in the workplace than bother trying to hire another employee to replace you. You see how simple it can be? Now, that isn't saying that you have a boss or employer this would work on,

Chapter 4: Mind Control

but if you are implementing the other tools you have in your fast-growing arsenal, you are now a very well-liked employee and co-worker who knows how to influence and persuade others to see things the way you do. Your employer may not like the idea of paying you even more than before, but sometimes it's not just your work ethic that matters, sometimes it's what you bring to the table for everyone you encounter.

It is not easy to say no to someone who you feel a debt to. The final technique of mood control we should consider is generosity. You should always strive to give more than you take from others. When you give more of your time, your effort, your attention, to others, they appreciate it. They remember it. And, when the time comes that you want something in return, it is much harder to say no, or disagree, or refuse to cooperate with another who has freely offered up so much to them. Even in circumstances or changes others may not want to agree or get on board with, if they know that you have been offered the same courtesy by you previously, they find it hard to go against you. It falls back to persuasion, influence, and reciprocation. Most often, those that you have committed your time and attention to will return the favor. Even if you are met with resistance by someone who you have given to, a gentle reminder of what you have done for them is often all that is needed to get them on board with what you want. Sometimes it isn't the loudest voice in the room that matters, but the most consistent and softest from the individual who has done the most to help others. That soft but firm voice can be yours, you only need to take your opportunities as they present themselves.

Chapter 5:

NLP (Neuro-Linguistic Programming)

We have delved into the art of persuasion, what it is, and how to start practicing your ability to persuading others. We have discussed how to understand others, and how understanding others can benefit you in your goals. We know that gaining and using influence to achieve our desires is possible. We have even discussed mind-control and many of its methods, and how to put these methods to everyday use. Now, we are digging deeper, into the world of Neuro-Linguistic Programming, or NLP for short.

Chapter 5: NLP (Neuro-Linguistic Programming)

NLP was founded and introduced by Richard Brandler and John Grinder in Santa Cruz, California in the 1970's amidst the Human Potential Movement. The Human Potential Movement was a psychotherapeutic movement that took a humanistic approach to people and their woes. The focus during this movement was personal psychological growth and understanding through many techniques. The most emphasized of these techniques were the use, application, and participation of encounter groups, sensitivity training, and primal therapy.

Encounter groups were a new way of thinking in the therapy world. Individuals participating in this type of therapy met as a group with a trainer to help guide their individual and collective process. Group sessions could last for hours, even days, and the length of the sessions was said to help members become uninhibited, literally exhausting its participants, allowing for an increase of self-awareness through verbal interactions that were not directed or influenced greatly by the trainer. Open displays of all range of emotions were welcomed and encouraged, even displays of rage, hostility, and grief.

Sensitivity training was encouraged to help people become more aware of their own prejudices, their own judgements and assumptions, and to become more sensitive and aware of others and their diversities within their group or workplace. Unstructured discussions amongst the group were encouraged to help increase empathy and embrace differences. This type of training is still popular and is often used within business and corporate models to increase harmony among employees and management.

Primal therapy was introduced by Dr. Arthur Janov. Dr. Janov believed that an individual's mental and physical ailments were a manifestation of repressed traumas, usually occurring in childhood. This type of treatment would begin with a patient seeing the therapist on-on-one for three weeks, concluding after

Chapter 5: NLP (Neuro-Linguistic Programming)

fifteen sessions, to explore and get to the root of past traumas and how to overcome them. After the initial one-on-one sessions were completed, the individual patient was introduced to group therapy sessions once to twice a week, with no conclusion or time frame for completion. The focus on these group sessions was to allow patients a safe environment to lose control of their feelings and emotions to process their pain with assistance in a controlled environment, therefore alleviating the effect the trauma's they experienced and the effect those traumatic events had on their overall mental and physical health and well-being.

Now that you have a background on the Human Potential Movement of the 1970's, you will be able to better appreciate the theories behind the introduction of NLP into the world of psychotherapy. The ideas behind NLP are interesting to say the least, and it is important to note that many have discredited the applications and effectiveness of NLP because of what is claimed to be a lack of hard data to support the theories, and the belief that most of the theories of NLP are based on hypothesis only, that is, educated guesses or assumptions made by Bandler and Grinder during their research. Despite the naysayers, NLP is still used as a tool by many self-help personalities, corporations, educators, and psychotherapists today, as well as coaches and for business and management training groups.

The psychotherapeutic applications of NLP are to use the basic principles as a tool to successfully achieve success during instances of persuasion, in negotiations (either in business or personal matters), and during public speaking. For an individual to master the art of NLP, much practice and training will be required to achieve positive results, as NLP demands much control and subtlety. In fact, there are quite a few online workshops and certificate programs available, as well as physical schools dedicated to educating, instructing, and helping those interested in

Chapter 5: NLP (Neuro-Linguistic Programming)

learning how to master the art of NLP. The theories behind NLP are very complex, and can be very hard for the layperson, or someone not familiar with the science and physiology behind the concepts of NLP to understand. In this book, we will introduce the principles and beliefs of what NLSP at is most basic concepts teaches, and how best a person being introduced to the concepts may begin to apply those concepts to achieve their desired goals.

Neuro-Linguistic Programming uses the premise that there is a connection between the language we speak, and the behavior patterns we all exhibit, and that both the way we speak, what words we use, and the way we normally behave can be altered or changed by other's who use NLP to achieve their own goals. That is, that a practitioner of NLP can change or alter another person's normal behaviors or thought patterns. Per the practitioners of NLP, our behavior is best understood based on our five senses, and that our perceptions of reality are subjective and different to everyone based on which of our senses is most prominent at the time of engagement, and that each person's ruling sensory interpretation changes regularly.

In easier terms, NLP states that linguistics (or language) is more than just words we speak, but also how our individual brains process and interpret these communications. Individual processing of this information is stressed, as another vital aspect of NLP is that no two people process and interpret information in the same way. Again, it is important to note that all five senses play a factor in our perception of our lives. So, in theory, by using the practices underlined in NLP, an individual's perception of their reality, their lives, can be altered for the better. Here it should be mentioned that not all people research and study NLP for the sole purpose of practicing NLP techniques on others, but also on themselves to better their life circumstances, or to change things they perceive to be negative in their lives.

Chapter 5: NLP (Neuro-Linguistic Programming)

To begin the practice of NLP on another person, the most valuable and important aspect is to begin to build a rapport with the other party, or to already have built rapport with the person in question. Rapport is a close relationship that includes mutual understanding of one another's feelings, and an ability to communicate well between yourself and the other party. Rapport is something that you have already built with a close friend or acquaintance, or a family member. When considering the requirements and steps that are needed to begin trying to practice the concepts of NLP on another person, other than already having a close relationship with said individual in question, your influence and the esteem or authority with which the other party views you are significant factors. It is much less difficult to build rapport with someone who looks up to you, sees you as a figure or authority, or defers to you and your knowledge.

So now that you have built rapport with another person, what's next?

The notion is to now begin layering very subtle meaning into your spoken or written interactions with the other person, to begin to implant suggestions in a very light and subconscious way. By stressing key words or phrases when communicating, you are highlighting these key words, and the other person's brain is subconsciously recognizing or remembering them without them being fully aware of what is occurring within their own body. Again, it is important to stress that subtlety is key. Another way to achieve the layered meanings you want to achieve is to use metaphors that can be interpreted in different ways, and the use of double-entendres. An example of a double-entendre was a very ironic and humorous quote by the late Hollywood actress Mae West. Mae once stated "Marriage is a fine institution, but I'm not ready for an institution.". What Mae was getting at is that while the institution of marriage is good and well for others that chose to get married, it also could make those that did marry crazy enough to be institutionalized. It is funny,

Chapter 5: NLP (Neuro-Linguistic Programming)

a play on words, and has a clear double meaning and is open for interpretation.

Emotional speaking, or talking about things that will illicit an emotional response within the other person is also very useful. Knowing what words, phrases, stories, or double-entendres will illicit an emotional response will depend upon how well you know the individual or group of person's you are speaking to. If you understand the other's motivation or the reason being why they want to listen to you. Speak to what you think will create emotion within them. What emotion do you want them to feel? What words make you feel the way you want them to feel? What words make you feel happy? Joy, fun, pleasure, satisfaction, glee, bliss, ecstasy, all are words that convey and illicit happiness. A great example of stimulating a specific emotion, the emotions of optimism and change were invoked in millions of American's during Barack Obama's presidential campaign. The simple phrase, "Yes We Can", along with the simplistic imagery used causes a nationwide emotional response. Simple, to the point, and very effective. When speaking to other's emotions, simple and short is the most effective way to create a specific response in others. The shorter a message is, the more likely the other party's brain will retain it. Our brains can only contain so much information at a time, and it is best to not overload another person with long winded speeches or dialogues. Make an impact. Stress a sentence or phrase that you know will produce the emotional response you hope it does, and then emphasize it by using similar words throughout the communication.

Now that you have built rapport with someone, and you are actively using subtle layering techniques, and speaking to the person's emotions, it is time to become very observant. Watch the tiny non-verbal cues the other party exhibits during this interaction to modify the way you speak to them. Are they moving their eyes away from you, looking at you directly,

Chapter 5: NLP (Neuro-Linguistic Programming)

rolling their eyes to the side? Is there any indication that you need to rephrase a sentence, or use alternative word choices based on how they react? Are their pupils dilating or constricting? Pupillary response is physiological and not a voluntary reaction that is controllable. Pupil dilation as it relates to emotional reaction may indicate sexual arousal, curiosity, or cognitive workload (as in, you are making them think). Pupil constriction can be a sign of a negative response, like fight-or-flight responses are being demonstrated in the body and it is time for you to re-direct the conversation, or disengage altogether and attempt your communication goals later. The faster a pupillary reaction occurs, the stronger their emotional response to the interaction is. Being able to notice pupillary response is something that is easy to practice on a day to day basis, but difficult to master.

Other non-verbal cues that need to be considered are flushing of the skin, their body language, and whether you feel they are being honest with their exchanges, or if there is any indication that they are falsifying certain details, giving false responses, or outright lying. Lying is hard work for the brain, so people who are not telling the truth must work harder at communicating as opposed to people that are being honest and open. People that are lying tend to leave small details out of their stories or responses, as it is easy to forget what specifics were given while lying. If someone mentions a concert they recently attended, but they leave out details or cannot recall what the opening set was, chances are, they aren't being honest. Memory, or the lack of one is another tale. Those that embellish or lie often claim to have a lacking memory, as it is harder to get caught up in a lie if you "can't remember" the information being asked. Correcting what is said is another easy way to tell if someone is not being honest, especially if the individual corrects themselves repeatedly during

Chapter 5: NLP (Neuro-Linguistic Programming)

the interaction. Contradicting information or statements is also a dead giveaway, as is being fidgety, seeming to be nervous or preoccupied, or tense. Just like watching pupil reaction and other non-verbal cues, it is all about keen observation of the overall physical response the other person is exhibiting. Observing other people on this level in an imperceptible way takes a lot of time and practice to master, but with time, your brain can quickly take note of another person's emotional reactions and non-verbal tales. This is important, because it enables you to be able to change their response or way of thinking by interpreting what they are thinking, how you are making them feel, and deciding how to best change their response or thinking to match your own.

The next step in implementing NLP strategies after you have carefully and strategically observed the other person or people, is to then begin to mimic them. By imitating the other persons, you are attempting to create

Persuasion

subconscious affiliation with them. This affiliation is another way for those individuals to feel a closer connection with you, as you are similar, even if it is a connection that is solely felt by your generation of it. Other important things to consider mirroring are their mannerisms, and their speech patterns. As mentioned previously, NLP is an art form that takes practice, less your efforts be noticed. If you are not subtle with your techniques, and another person realizes that you are taking on their own affects, they will immediately feel as though you are mocking or imitating them, and many see this as a negative and extremely offensive. Remember, the goal is to get them to trust you, to see you as an ally, someone they could easily have a meaningful connection with, not some hack that is fake or false in their interactions.

Once a rapport has been built, and you have observed non-verbal social queues, created an emotional and significant bond by your design through subtle simulation, it is time to put all

Chapter 5: NLP (Neuro-Linguistic Programming)

your efforts to use. Allow and encourage the other person to talk about themselves, and continuing to be engaged. At the same time, you need to allow the other party to see a sense of openness and vulnerability within yourself, in a real and honest way. It has been stated before, and is now being reiterated again, that people sense falseness, and being fake in your interactions and willingness to be open to them in turn will be admonished. So, by engaging another party or group of people with this give and take will allow an opportunity, created by your own hard work and practices, for others to trust you and what you have to say. Gaining that trust is paramount, as it allows you to begin to steer the conversation in the direction you wish it to go. Steering other's thoughts in the direction you desire allows you the opportunity to set up the exchange to your benefit, and ultimately, gives you the upper hand in getting what you want, persuading others that your ideas or goals are the most logical and accurate, and that you want what everyone else wants too.

Persuasion

Remember to elicit emotional states and responses in others as you continue to steer the scenario. Anchoring, again, slight nuanced touch to the upper arm in a natural and quick fashion only furthers your goal. And your goal is easier reached when following these practices that the NLP techniques offers you.

Chapter 6:

Reflect on Yourself

So far, we have delved into the world of persuasion, and how to get what you want out of life by learning how to understand others for your own benefit, using influence to sway people to see things your way, and how to use simple and not-so-simple mind control and NLP techniques to achieve your goals. But what about you? What do you want out of life? Are you satisfied with all aspects of your world, or could you use a little help persuading yourself to make changes?

This chapter is all about you.

Do you understand yourself well? Do you know who you truly are and what makes you happy? Do you need help achieving what you want? Are

Chapter 6: Reflect on Yourself

you completely self-aware? To make any lasting changes to your own life, you need to know everything you can about you. Sometimes, a little insight into your own psyche goes a long way. Often our own subconscious thoughts and desires aren't apparent. Our actions and choices are often influenced by our subconscious. In order to reach the ultimate self-awareness, understanding all we can about ourselves is key. Sometimes we know exactly how we feel, precisely what we want, but that isn't always the case. There are many ways we can help ourselves learn more, or at least gain a deeper understanding about our inner-most wants or yearnings, and how to change what we are unsatisfied with.

Often, we need others to hold the mirror up for us to see things about who we are more clearly. It helps to focus more on what is present, what it is we need to concentrate on to help us achieve betterment, and not trying to accomplish this task while holding the mirror ourselves allows us more room to focus on the big picture. An objective opinion about what makes us tick can be a priceless jewel when reaching for our best self. Psychoanalysis is one way to achieve this objective view into our psyche. Another good tool for self-discovery may be taking career tests, discovering how we learn best (learning style), or taking personality tests and quizzes.

To reach your full potential, you need to know who you are, warts and all, and what makes you tick. What motivates us is just as important as learning what motivates others. Do you value security over adventure? What are you good at? What are your weaknesses? What is the best thing about you? What in your life gives you joy, and what are you unhappy with? Answering these questions is a good start to understanding yourself.

When making choices, do you think about the consequences, are you logical, always weighing cause and effect, or do your base choice on emotion? Considering that we have all probably

Chapter 6: Reflect on Yourself

based decisions on both the logical choice and our emotions, it becomes clear that with each choice we make, something deeper often lies just below. Consider major events in your life, both good and bad, and how they impacted you in the moment. Are these events still impacting your choices today? Self-evaluation can only help you realize your aspirations.

Do you know that you can persuade and influence yourself to change your mind and improve your life? Self-persuasion is not difficult once you make friends with your true identity and nature. Self-evaluation can be hard at times. We don't always have the best attitudes or ideals, and our priorities aren't always the healthiest for bettering life circumstances. But, once you grasp the big picture on who you are, knowing that YOU CAN CHOOSE TO CHANGE anything you want in your own life is an empowering idea. The task can seem daunting if there are many areas you are unsatisfied with, but you can choose how you tackle making changes.

Starting with your biggest motivator helps many reach their goals. Other people need to see results quickly to become motivated, and so they choose to start with small or easier things to focus on. Whichever direction you choose to use as your starting point, moving forward is the most important step. Reminding yourself daily that some changes do not occur overnight will help keep you focused and prevent feeling frustrated, therefore, giving up too quickly. Looking forward to achieving the change you wish is a positive future outlook and will only help to further change and better your attitude and current viewpoint. Beginning to focus not on what is wrong, but what is right or will be corrected moving forward is possible. To focus your energy on your present accomplishment and further achievement, stop negative and backward thoughts. The point of making a change is not to continually think back on what

Chapter 6: Reflect on Yourself

you don't want, but rather redirecting those negative notions by stopping that train of thought, and going back to the future and what it will look like.

Another way to aid yourself in self-persuasion is to use visual reminders of what your end-goal is. Just like the chubby kid that takes photos of healthy and fit people and posts them on the refrigerator to help motivate and remind them what their end goal is (to lose weight and exercise), visual aids can help keep your goal fresh in your mind. Although the example given is more a negative motivator than a positive one, it can work for you in a similar way. If you want to make more money, envision how you would like to get there, and what your life will look like once you achieve that success. Create a vision board for yourself to look at, save pictures of your ideal, and remind yourself that anyone is possible of anything with work, even you. Daydream about your goal, work on imagining how you will feel when you have accomplished what you desire. Surround yourself with like-minded individuals who share the same goals as you, or with people who support you in reaching for what you want. If you are trying to get healthier or fit, find friends or family who are working towards physical betterment as well, or network with people that already possess the physical health you are working towards. You do not have time to entertain negative people or pessimists who do not support you. Remember, the entire point of making a change is to better your life. Anyone who does not wish you well on your journey and support you does not have your best interests at heart.

A useful tool of NLP that you can use on yourself is to begin re-programming negativity to your advantage. The reason this is a good idea, is that often the fear of failure, or a fear of the unknown, stops one from making positive changes because of the negative connotation that one may feel. You stop yourself before you even start, simply because you do not wish to experience an

Chapter 6: Reflect on Yourself

unpleasant emotion or feeling. Unfortunately, growing pains are a real thing, and negative emotions or physical discomfort are often a part of the process towards betterment. So, what is a way that you can use discomfort or negative feelings to your advantage? And how can you re-program your own mind to overcome these feelings, maybe even come to embrace them?

To start, choose the goal you want to achieve. Think about how you want to reach the goal in question, and the steps you will need to take in order to do so. Now, what is your biggest fear associated with this goal? Or, what causes you to worry or stop yourself from taking the leap and going for it? Focus on that undesirable emotion or action, imagine it is happening now. The idea is to physically induce the experience now, not when it occurs in the future. Yes, the idea of making yourself feel negativity sounds unpleasant, and it is. But you need to feel this way now, because you are going to learn how to master this unpleasantness.

Once you feel this fear, or pain, or embarrassment, whatever negative feeling or emotion that is holding you back, you need to begin to imagine that this thing you are avoiding is in front of you. It is not just an internal reaction, but a physical manifestation that has a life of its own. Imagine what it looks like, how it moves. Does it look like something and have a form, or is it like a cloud or other abstract shape? Do you associate a smell or color with this thing in front of you? You need to be very clear on what this thing is, taking your time until you not only experience the emotions that it elicits within you, but you see in your mind exactly what it is and what it looks like. Now you are facing your fear. Kill it. How you kill or defeat it does not matter. You can will it to disappear or simply go away from you, you can stomp on it, use a sword. This is your fear, your imagination, and you can dispose of what you do not wish any way you see fit. Have fun with sending your negativity away from you, but be clear on how you accomplish this. Just as you have detailed what this fear

Chapter 6: Reflect on Yourself

looks like, so to do you need to be very clear and consistent with how you get rid of it.

You just killed the fear, worry, anxiety, or whatever adverse emotion or feeling was holding you back. It is gone. Dead. How do you feel? Feel your emotions, and your physical body. Focus on how every separate finger and toe feels, how your skin feels, your arms, legs, scan your entire body and relax every muscle. This activity is also referred to as grounding yourself, and creates a calm and relaxed overall feeling. The negative things that hold you back are now away from you, and you feel at peace. While in this state of relaxation and calm, think of a few ways you can deal with this negative emotion or situation if it arises again in day to day life, and how you can overcome or solve this instance as it happens in real time. Once you have settled on how to beat these worries, write it down on paper to cement it in your mind. Imagine defeating it repeatedly, following the process outlined here as often as you need to. Refer to your written resolutions and ways to solve these problems. They become smaller to you. The thing you fear, or what is holding you back, is no longer huge and menacing, but becomes a small and insignificant issue as you continue to re-program your mind and retrain the way you see and deal with adversity.

As you can clearly see, NLP is a very effective concept, and it can not only be used as an advantageous technique that will help you understand and redirect others for your benefit, but a tool with which you can better your own life and circumstance. As with all the topics we have gone over in this book, practice makes perfect. Utilizing this exercise whenever you can will only make you better at it. The better you are at facing and excising your doubts, worries, uncertainties and concerns, the less they impact your choices, decisions, and actions.

Conclusion

You can achieve any goal, see all your ambitions come to fruition, and overcome any obstacle that you want to. Understanding people is the key to realizing your goals. Whether you want to persuade another person to agree with your viewpoint, influence and build rapport with colleagues, or change the way someone sees a topic through the powers of suggestion using mind control techniques, you now have a basic understanding of how to achieve success using the skills and tools outlined in this book. Persuasion and influence are powerful tools that every successful person possesses, and you can be one of those people. You are the captain of your ship, and you can determine not only where you go, but also how you get there, and who takes the journey with you.

Conclusion

The next step to seeing your ambitions realized is to practice what you know. No successful person became the best version of themselves overnight. It takes time, preparation, and repetition to master your skills. Making your new abilities a habit is possible. Give yourself time to put into practice what you now know. No large goal is ever easy to attain, but all goals are achievable if you decide that not only is this what you want, but that you will prevail. You oversee your own life. You are the one who dictates your success, and you can persuade and influence others that not only are you right, but that they are right as well, because they see that you want what is best for everyone. You just have only to make up your mind, and go for it!

Remember that the art of NLP, persuasion, influence and understanding are not only used for the sole purpose of changing others opinions or minds, but your own as well. Understanding who you really are, what you think and feel, and why you feel the way you do only aids in your ability to understand where other people are coming from. And, knowing yourself inside out will help you see what is most important to you, what your priorities are, and any changes that you need to make in order to see your dreams realized. You are capable of anything, and you can make your life exactly what you want it to be.

Thank you again for wanting to master the power you have within yourself, and for taking the time to read the information provided to help you gain a new understanding of how to go about getting everything you aspire and aim for out of life. Finally, if you found this book useful in anyway, a review on Amazon is always greatly appreciated!

www.ingramcontent.com/pod-product-compliance
Lightning Source LLC
Chambersburg PA
CBHW052104110526
44591CB00013B/2344